Taylor Swift
FEARLESS

S0-AAZ-601

HAL•LEONARD® CORPORATION

7777 W. BLUEMOUND RD. P.O. BOX 13819 MILWAUKEE, WI 53213

Visit Hal Leonard Online at
www.halleonard.com

FEARLESS

Words and Music by TAYLOR SWIFT,
LIZ ROSE and HILLARY LINDSEY

Moderately

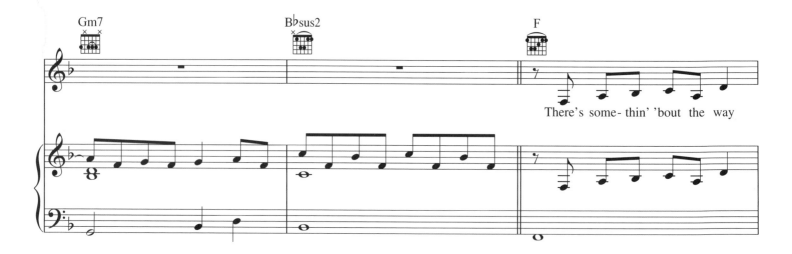

There's some- thin' 'bout the way

the street looks when it's just rained. There's a glow off the pave - ment. You walk me to the

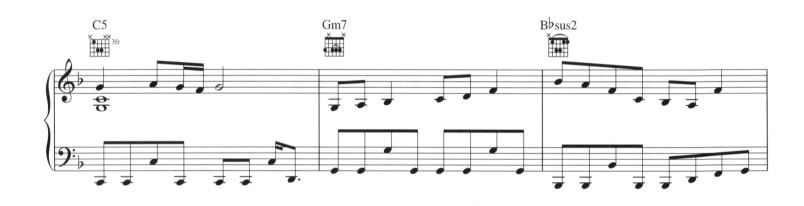

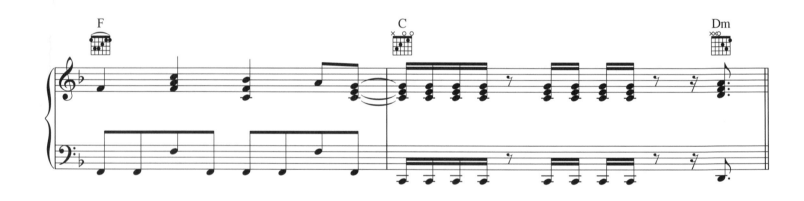

Well, you stood ___ there with me _____ in the door - way, my hands _

FIFTEEN

Words and Music by
TAYLOR SWIFT

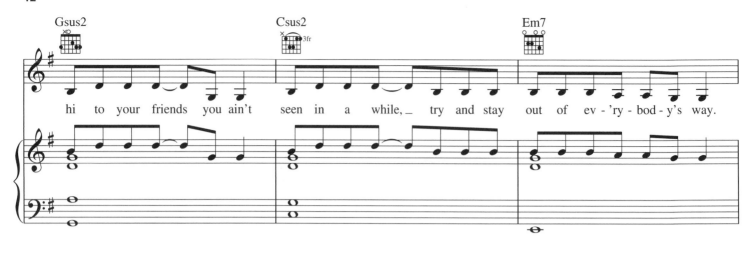

hi to your friends you ain't seen in a while, __ try and stay out of ev-'ry-bod-y's way.

It's your fresh-man year and you're

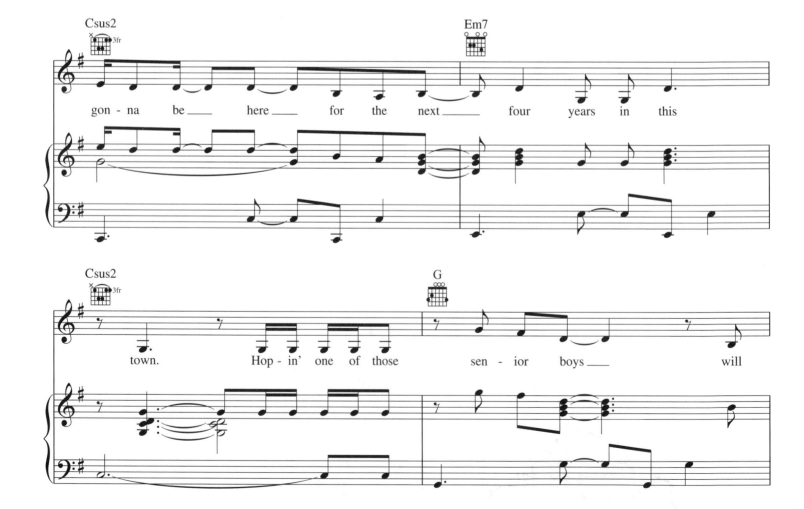

gon-na be __ here __ for the next __ four years in this

town. Hop-in' one of those sen-ior boys __ will

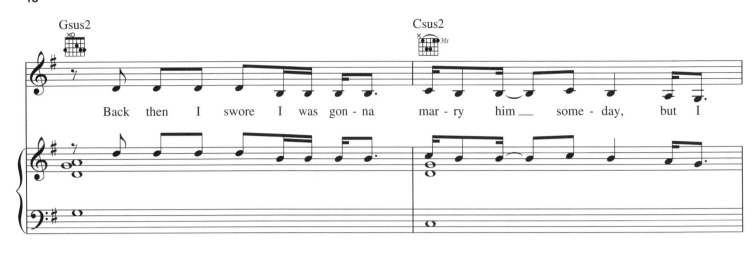

Back then I swore I was gon-na mar-ry him ___ some-day, but I

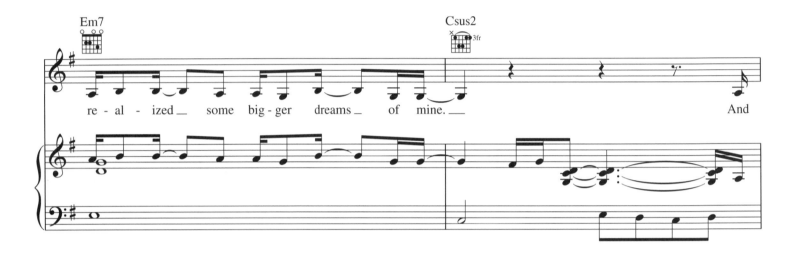

re - al - ized __ some big-ger dreams __ of mine. __ And

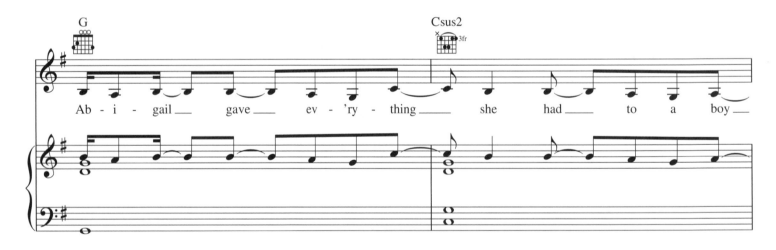

Ab - i - gail __ gave __ ev - 'ry - thing __ she had __ to a boy __

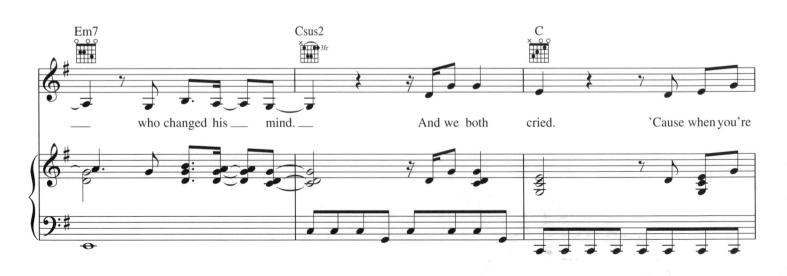

__ who changed his __ mind. __ And we both cried. 'Cause when you're

LOVE STORY

Words and Music by
TAYLOR SWIFT

Moderately

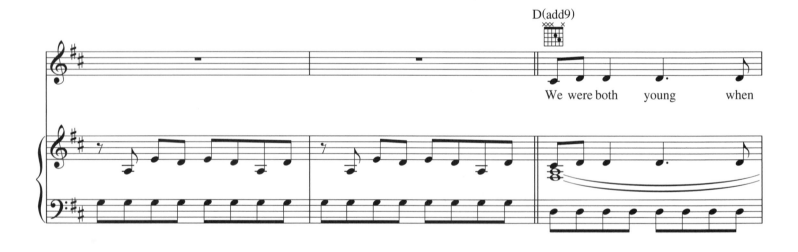

We were both young when

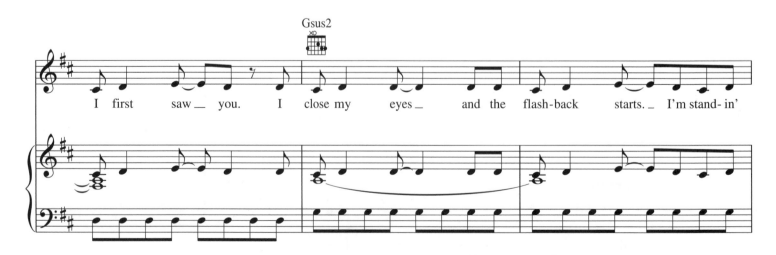

I first saw you. I close my eyes and the flash-back starts. I'm stand-in'

HEY STEPHEN

Words and Music by
TAYLOR SWIFT

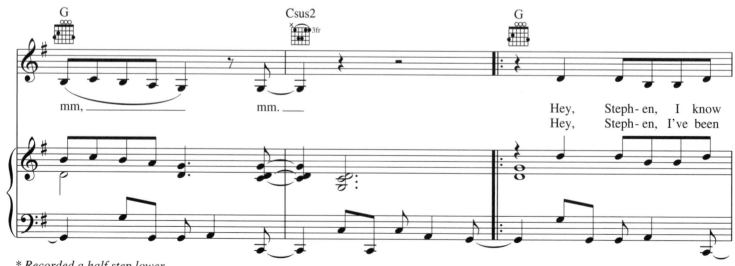

Recorded a half step lower.

36

WHITE HORSE

Words and Music by TAYLOR SWIFT
and LIZ ROSE

YOU BELONG WITH ME

Words and Music by TAYLOR SWIFT
and LIZ ROSE

Recorded a half step lower.

BREATHE

Words and Music by TAYLOR SWIFT
and COLBIE CAILLAT

Moderately

I see your face in my mind as I drive a-way 'cause

Recorded a half step lower.

breathe _____ with - out ____ you, ____

but I have to.

TELL ME WHY

Words and Music by TAYLOR SWIFT
and LIZ ROSE

YOU'RE NOT SORRY

Words and Music by
TAYLOR SWIFT

Lyrics:

All this time I was wast-in', hop-in' you would come a-round.

look-in' so in-no-cent I might be-lieve you if I did-n't know.

I've been giv-in' out chanc-es ev-'ry time and all you do is let ___

Could-'ve loved you all my life ___ if you had-n't left me wait-in' in ___

*Recorded a half step lower.

You had me crawl-in' for you, hon-ey, and it nev-er would've gone a-way,____ no.____ You used to shine so bright, but I watched all of it fade.____

THE WAY I LOVED YOU

Words and Music by TAYLOR SWIFT
and JOHN RICH

FOREVER AND ALWAYS

Words and Music by
TAYLOR SWIFT

THE BEST DAY

Words and Music by
TAYLOR SWIFT

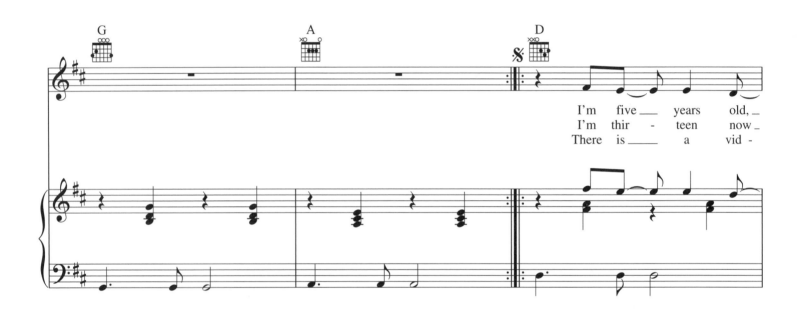

I'm five ___ years old,
I'm thir - teen now
There is ___ a vid -

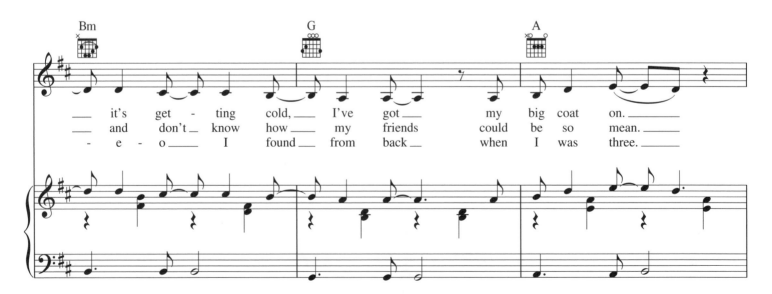

___ it's get - ting cold, ___ I've got ___ my big coat on. ___
___ and don't ___ know how ___ my friends could be so mean. ___
- e - o ___ I found ___ from back ___ when I was three. ___

*Recorded a half step lower.

CHANGE

Words and Music by
TAYLOR SWIFT

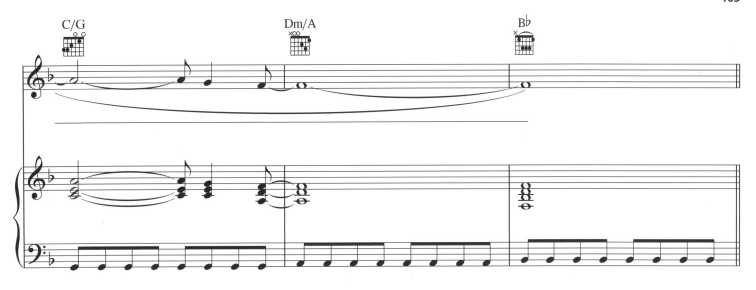

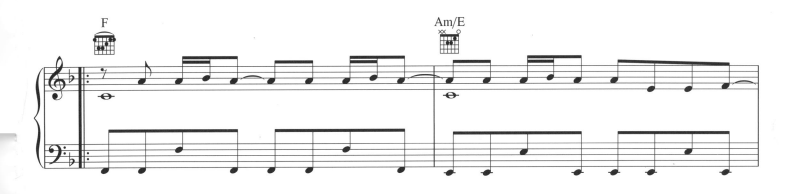

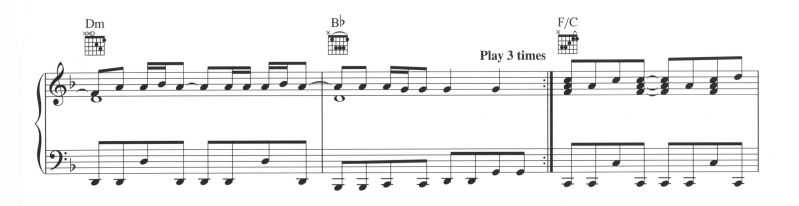

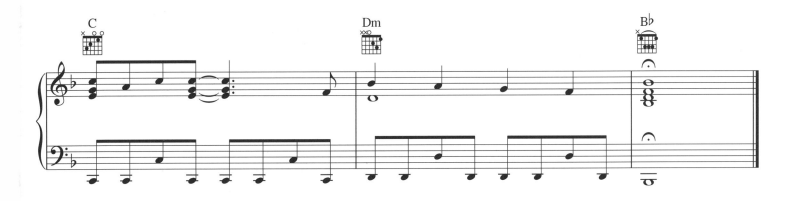